U0065803

心之道

Self-restraint
Establishing guidelines
which support the practice

建立學佛生活軌則

第三輯

心道法師 語錄
By Dharma
Master Hsin Tao

目錄

Contents

Self-restraint :
Establishing guidelines which
support the practice

　　心道法師一九四八年生，祖籍雲南，幼失依怙，為滇緬邊境孤雛。十三歲隨孤軍撤移來台，十五歲初聞觀音菩薩聖號，有感於觀音菩薩的悲願，以「悟性報觀音」、「吾不成佛誓不休」、「真如度眾生」刺身供佛，立誓

徹悟真理，救度苦難。

二十五歲出家後，
頭陀行腳歷十餘年，前
後在台北外雙溪、宜
蘭礁溪圓明寺、莿仔崙
墳塔、龍潭公墓和員
山周舉人廢墟，體驗
世間最幽隱不堪的「塚
間修」，矢志修證，了
脫生死，覺悟本來。

生道場」，展開弘法度
生的佛行事業，為現代
人擘劃成佛地圖。為了
推動宗教共存共榮，法
師以慈悲的華嚴理念奔
走國際，並於二○○一
年十一月成立世界宗教
博物館，致力於各種不
同宗教的對話，提昇對
所有宗教的寬容、尊重

9

著重基礎佛法戒、定、
慧的學習與薰陶，建立
佛法生活規範；「般若
期」著重在明瞭與貫徹
空性智慧；「法華期」
著重生起願力，發菩提
心；「華嚴期」則強調
多元共存、和諧共生，
證入圓滿無礙的境界。

　　心道法師以禪的

Brief Introduction to the Author

Born in upper Myanmar in 1948 to ethnic Chinese parents of Yunnan Province, Master Hsin Tao was left orphaned and impoverished at an early age. Having

Self-restraint
Establishing guidelines which
support the practice

been taken in by
the remnants of
ROC military units
operating along the
border of Yunnan,
China, he was brought
to Taiwan in 1961
when he was 13. At
the age of 15, he was

the Buddha, he had
himself tattooed
with the vows
"May I awaken
in gratitude for
the kindness of
Guanyin," "I will
never rest until
Buddhahood is

Self-restraint
Establishing guidelines which
support the practice

enlightenment,
Master Hsin Tao
traveled on foot
for over ten years,
practicing austerities
in lonely and secluded
locations, including
Waishuangxi in
Taipei, Yuanming

the Fahua Cave on
Fulong Mountain in
early 1983, Master
Hsin Tao undertook
a fast which was to
last over two years,
during which time
he attained deep
insight into the

Self-restraint
Establishing guidelines which
support the practice

Master Hsin Tao felt
great compassion
for the suffering of
all sentient beings.
After his solitary
retreat he established
the Wusheng Monastery
on the mountain in
order to propagate

strived hard to
gain international
support with the
compassionate spirit
of the Buddhist
Avatamsaka Vision (of
the interconnectedness
of all beings in
the universe), and

is dedicated to
advancing the cause
of world peace
and a promoting
awareness of our
global family for
love and peace
through interreligious
dialogues. The

practice. First comes
the āgama stage,
which centers on
the foundational
teachings of Buddhism
and the three-fold
practice of morality,
concentration, and
wisdom. The prajñā

Self-restraint
Establishing guidelines which
support the practice

stage emphasizes the
theory and practice
of emptiness. The
dharmapuṇḍarīka
stage focuses on the
bodhisattva practice
of developing the
mind of enlightenment
through the power

Master Hsin Tao
has devoted himself
to propagating the
Dharma through
education, based on
the Chan principle
of quieting the mind
and seeing one's
original Buddha-

Self-restraint
Establishing guidelines which
support the practice

律己篇 智慧法語

commitment, he
leads people to
devote themselves
to the great cause
of benefiting all
sentient beings,
ceaselessly helping
them achieve liberating
truth   through

心之道第三輯 智慧法語

律己篇-建立學佛生活軌則

The Way of Mind III:
Words of wisdom

Self-restraint :
Establishing guidelines which
support the practice

學佛
要從思想開始清淨，
然後用到生活上，
行為也清淨。

Purity begins
with the mind,
and then extends into
daily life.

禪就是攝心與明心。

Chan
is to rein in
and enlighten the mind.

沒有任何一樣事物是
可得的，
不要去執著任何事物，
要慢慢養成
無所得的心。

Ultimately,
there's nothing to attain ;
don't cling to anything;
gradually cultivate
the spirit of no attainment.

在感情上用功的人，
等於是在水中撈月、
在假象上用心，
永遠都是痛苦的。

Self-restraint
Establishing guidelines which
support the practice

Grasping at emotions
is like trying to
catch an image of the moon
reflected in water;
getting caught up
in figments of the
imagination always
results in suffering.

Self-restraint
Establishing guidelines which
support the practice

Practicing Buddhism
means training the mind;
only after
you've trained
your own mind
is it possible
to train others.

Life sprouts forth
from the seeds of karma.

禪就是
簡單、自然、
樸實、和諧。

Self-restraint
Establishing guidelines which
support the practice

Chan is all about
simplicity, naturalness,
sincerity, and harmony.

Self-restraint
Establishing guidelines which
support the practice

Following the Noble
Eightfold Path,
you encounter the suffering
which leads to the end of
suffering.

能夠隨時隨地
降伏自己，
就是最快樂的人。

The person
who never loses self-control
— this is
a truly happy person.

以「五戒十善」
為身、口、意結界，
回到心源自性。

Self-restraint
Establishing guidelines which
support the practice

Keeping your
actions of body, speech,
and mind within the bounds
prescribed by the five precepts
and the ten wholesome
courses of action, you return
to the source of the mind
— your self-nature.

Self-restraint
Establishing guidelines which
support the practice

Practicing Buddhism means
transforming discrimination
and attachment into
wisdom.

「戒」是
讓一切具足善法；
「定」是
調伏自己的心；
「慧」是
觀照一切真實。

"Morality" means
refraining from all forms of
unwholesome conduct;
"concentration" means
bringing the mind
under control;
"wisdom" means observing
everything as it really is.

苦是我們出離的因，
我們要離苦，
要時時刻刻看到苦。

We use suffering to
transcend suffering;
being fully aware of
suffering at all times
leads to
the end of suffering.

心念是
由「相」組合而成；
生死是
由「業」組合而成。

Self-restraint
Establishing guidelines which
support the practice

律己篇
智慧法語

Thoughts arise
from sense impressions;
saṃsāra arises
from karma.

有「定」以後，
才能夠照明很多現象，
智慧才會生起來。

Self-restraint
Establishing guidelines which
support the practice

Once concentration is
established
you can see things clearly;
only then is it possible
for wisdom to arise.

This is how to rein
in the mind:
Bring your attention from
the eyes to the nose,
from the nose to the mouth,
and from the mouth to the
heart. There are no images
in your heart.

Self-restraint
Establishing guidelines which
support the practice

The Buddha-Dharma is not
mere theory; rather,
it's a practice.
It's the integration of
knowing and doing.

Only by drawing near
the spiritual teacher
do you come to return to
your true self,
understand saṃsāra, and
end all of your troubles.

「歇」即菩提，
讓你的心歇，
休歇即是菩提。

Self-restraint
Establishing guidelines which
support the practice

"Cessation" means
enlightenment; when
the mind comes to rest,
that is enlightenment.

Desire and attachment go
hand in hand;
when they come to an end,
what remains is purity.

閱讀經典，
讓我們清楚、明瞭
佛的方法，
而能在生活中實踐。

Self-restraint
Establishing guidelines which
support the practice

By reading the scriptures
we come to clearly
understand the Buddha's
teaching and how to put it
into practice in daily life.

Self-restraint
Establishing guidelines which
support the practice

When confronted with
karmic obstructions,
repentance practice is
the only way out.

Self-restraint
Establishing guidelines which
support the practice

律己篇
智慧法語

The five precepts and
the ten wholesome courses
of action are the foundation
of Buddhist practice.

注意每個念頭，
人跟人的相處，
寧可自己吃虧，
也不要佔人家的便宜。

Pay close attention to
your every thought and
how you interact with
people. Face setbacks
willingly, and never take
advantage of others.

Self-restraint
Establishing guidelines which
support the practice

Ignorance means
confusion and attachment;
wisdom is the only thing
that can dispel it.

心念種子必須清淨
才能斷煩惱,
「定」就是讓種子
一個個地不作用。

Self-restraint
Establishing guidelines which
support the practice

Only by purifying
the seeds of the mind is it
possible to cut off troubles.
When concentration is
strong, these seeds
lose their force.

外在的一切現象
就像「詐騙集團」，
人一不小心就容易被詐騙，
找不到自己的心，
看不到真正的自己。

Self-restraint
Establishing guidelines which
support the practice

The phenomenal world
is like a fraud ring.
If you're not careful,
it can easily fool you,
so that you lose sight of
your mind and lose touch
with your true self.

If you want to practice
seriously in daily life,
then you have to
uphold the precepts.

Self-restraint
Establishing guidelines which
support the practice

Life is impermanent and
full of tribulation;
you have to be mindful and
resolute.

苦行就是
淨化自己的心,
不要貪享樂、貪富貴。

Self-restraint
Establishing guidelines which
support the practice

Practicing austerities
brings about purification
of the mind; don't covet
wealth, status, or sensory
pleasures.

Self-restraint
Establishing guidelines which
support the practice

The arising and ceasing of
thoughts is saṃsāra;
by using listening to rein in
your thoughts,
you get in touch with
tranquility and emptiness.

When our thoughts are
wholesome,
tranquility arises
as a matter of course;
when our thoughts are
unwholesome,
we can't experience
much peace.

想要控制、轉換習氣，
就要專心持咒、
念佛、禪修。

Self-restraint
Establishing guidelines which
support the practice

Controlling and
transforming habitual
tendencies requires
wholeheartedly chanting
mantras, recollecting
the Buddha, and
practicing meditation.

當下
就把每個「因」做好，
每個來到眼前的「緣」，
無論好壞
都如同還給你一份加持。

Self-restraint
Establishing guidelines which
support the practice

Whatever you properly
attend to
in the present moment
comes back to you later
as a blessing — or as a
blessing in disguise.

日常生活中，
時常清理染著，
可以讓業障變輕、
執著變少，
心就相對輕鬆。

In the midst of daily life,
by continually clearing
away defilements,
you lessen attachments, and
lighten your karmic
obstructions; doing so,
you feel relaxed at heart.

生活中行八正道；
生活中跟隨三寶；
自然就會在生活中
產生無上的福田。

Self-restraint
Establishing guidelines which
support the practice

Daily life is the right place
for practicing
the Eightfold Noble Path
and for honoring
the Triple Gem;
in this way
all aspects of life become
a supreme field of merit.

執著越少，煩惱越輕；
執著越多，煩惱越重。

Self-restraint
Establishing guidelines which
support the practice

The stronger the attachment,
the stronger the troubles;
the weaker the attachment,
the weaker the troubles.

學佛，
必須超越貪、瞋、癡，
能夠超越，
就能由凡入聖。

Practicing Buddhism means
striving to overcome greed,
hatred, and delusion;
one who has completely
transcended them is known
as a saint.

是誰
讓我們的心不自由呢？
就是自己！
要學習自我解套。

Self-restraint
Establishing guidelines which
support the practice

Who has robbed you
of your freedom?
None other than yourself.
You have to learn
how to break free
from your self-created
bondage.

Self-restraint
Establishing guidelines which
support the practice

律己篇
智慧法語

Recollection of the Buddha
means waking up;
the Buddha's teaching
helps us to overcome
the pain of impermanence.

Self-restraint
Establishing guidelines which
support the practice

Upholding the precepts purifies
the karmic impressions which
keep us bound to the wheel
of life and death; through the
combined force of compassion
and wholesome affinities, these
impressions can be transformed
into wholesome seeds.

Self-restraint
Establishing guidelines which
support the practice

Spiritual practice requires
taming the mind and
making energetic striving
into a form of worship.

Self-restraint
Establishing guidelines which
support the practice

When faced with a problem,
don't react emotionally or
seek consolation;
in any difficult situation,
the Buddha-Dharma
is your greatest resource!

把生活環境整理乾淨，
內心就會舒適乾淨。

Self-restraint
Establishing guidelines which
support the practice

律己篇
智慧法語

A clean and tidy
living space
is conducive to
peace of mind.

將思想脈絡安住於
「正見」，
生活就會過得
四平八穩。

Self-restraint
Establishing guidelines which
support the practice

When all your thoughts
are guided by right view,
everything will be
smooth sailing.

起信，
道心才能堅固不退轉。

Self-restraint
Establishing guidelines which
support the practice

Arousing faith and
the aspiration for enlightenment
keeps you straight on the path
and precludes the possibility of
backsliding.

Self-restraint
Establishing guidelines which
support the practice

Preoccupation with prestige
is a hindrance;
spiritual practice
is all about discarding
hindrances.

一切的物質唯心所造，
所有的言行、思緒
都在造作自己的
「命」與「運」。

Everything is
a product of the mind;
through thoughts, words,
and deeds, we create
our own destiny.

平日多學習、
多聽佛法、閱讀佛經，
腦袋瓜就會靈活。

Self-restraint
Establishing guidelines which
support the practice

Reading the scriptures and
listening to Dharma talks
on a daily basis makes
the mind more agile.

Self-restraint
Establishing guidelines which
support the practice

Bickering is
the greatest suffering;
the absence of troubles is
the greatest miracle.

心之道第三輯智慧法語
律己篇-建立學佛生活軌則

心道法師語錄

總 策 劃：釋了意
主 編：洪淑妍
責任編輯：林玉芬
英文翻譯：甘修慈
英文審校：Dr. Maria Reis Habito
美術設計：蒲思元
發 行 人：歐陽慕親
出版發行：財團法人靈鷲山般若文教基金會附設出版社
劃撥帳戶：財團法人靈鷲山般若文教基金會附設出版社
劃撥帳號：18887793
地址：23444新北市永和區保生路2號21樓
電話：(02)2232-1008
傳真：(02)2232-1010
網址：www.093books.com.tw
讀者信箱：books@ljm.org.tw
法律顧問：永然聯合法律事務所
印刷：大亞彩色印刷製版股份有限公司
初版一刷：2014年7月
定價：新台幣250元(1套4冊)
ISBN：978-986-6324-76-5
總 經 銷：飛鴻國際行銷股份有限公司

靈鷲山書網

The Way of Mind Ⅲ : Words of wisdom
Self-restraint : Establishing guidelines which support the practice

Words of Dharma Master Hsin Tao

General Planer: Ven.Liao Yi Shih

Editor in Chief: Hong, Shu-yan

Editor in Charge: Lin, Yu-fen

English Translator: Gan, Xiu-hui

English Proofreading: Dr. Maria Reis Habito

Art Editor: Pu, Szu-Yuan

Publisher: Ouyang, Mu-qin

Published by and The postal service is allocated: the Subsidiary Publishing House of the Ling Jiou Mountain Prajna Cultural Education Foundation

Account Number: 18887793

Address: 21F., No.2, Baosheng Rd., Yonghe Dist., New Taipei City 23444, Taiwan (R.O.C.)

Tel: (02)2232-1008

Fax: (02)2232-1010

Website: www.093books.com.tw

E-mail: books@ljm.org.tw

Legal Consultant: Y. R. Lee & Partners Attorneys at Law

Printing: Apex Printing Corporation

The First Printing of the First Edition: July 2014

List Price: NT$ 250 dollars(Four-Manual Set)

ISBN: 978-986-6324-76-5

Distributor: Flying Horn International Marketing Co., Ltd.

國家圖書館出版品預行編目(CIP)資料

心之道智慧法語. 第三輯 / 洪淑妍主編.--初版.
-- 新北市：靈鷲山般若出版, 2014.07
　　冊；　　公分
ISBN 978-986-6324-76-5(全套：精裝)

1.佛教說法 2.佛教教化法

225.4　　　　　　　　　　　　　103011796